Let Us Pray

Let Us Pray

120 Prayers for All Occasions

David Clowes

transforming lives together

LET US PRAY
Published by David C Cook
4050 Lee Vance View
Colorado Springs, CO 80918 U.S.A.

David C Cook Distribution Canada
55 Woodslee Avenue, Paris, Ontario, Canada N3L 3E5

David C Cook U.K., Kingsway Communications
Eastbourne, East Sussex BN23 6NT, England

David C Cook and the graphic circle C logo
are registered trademarks of Cook Communications Ministries.

The Web site addresses recommended throughout this book
are offered as a resource to you. These Web sites are not
intended in any way to be or imply an endorsement on the part
of David C Cook, nor do we vouch for their content.

All Scripture quotations are taken from the Holy Bible, New
International Version®, NIV®. Copyright © 1973, 1978,
1984 by Biblica, Inc™. Used by permission of Zondervan.
All rights reserved worldwide. www.zondervan.com.

LCCN 2006933182
ISBN 978-1-56292-704-2

Selections printed in this book were previously published as *500
More Prayers for All Occasions* in 2003 by David C Cook.

Cover Design: Sarah Schultz
Cover Photo: iStockphoto
Interior Design: Karen Athen

Printed in the United States of America
First Edition 2007

2 3 4 5 6 7 8 9 10

100410

Contents

Introduction

Providing the people of God with the words and phrases with which to talk to their Maker is both a serious and a challenging task. In writing this book of prayers I set some guidelines. First, I aimed for simplicity of language and for a direct style of writing. I have attempted to write as I speak. I believe that this is important if the prayers are to be "prayed" and not simply read.

Second, I have tried to use as much nonchurch language as possible. This is important if the prayers are to be fresh and accessible to the widest possible group of people. It is vital that the language is neither too trendy nor too obscure but truly inclusive. Everyone should feel able to say a meaningful amen!

Third, I have never used any book of prayers just as they were written, and I expect this book will be used in the same way. Some of the prayers need to be used with care and a good deal of "space" and silence. Some, you will find, are like word portraits in the first person. The reader is then given a time of silence to pray for those they know to be in that situation. Some of the prayers invite readers to think of someone facing a particular experience. Again, time and silence in using these will be important.

I have presented eight categories of prayer. They offer a selection of prayers designed to prepare the readers for worship, to lift them up in praise, to provide an opportunity for thanksgiving, and to lead them into confession.

I think it would be true to say that the prayers in this book have been born out of my twenty-five years of pastoral work as a Methodist minister. They contain echoes of the hurt and the anguish, the hopes and the fears, the brokenness and the joy of the remarkable people it has been my privilege to know. I have always felt profoundly touched and humbled by the way others have allowed me to share in their journey. I can only say thank you and trust that the echoes from these pages will bless them too.

Writing these prayers opened a new door for me into the presence of God. I truly believe that they are his gift to me and to you. My prayer now is many will also be brought nearer to the throne of grace.

Prayers of Preparation

1

WHAT WE BRING

Lord, we come with our lives, our thoughts, our hopes, and our fears.

We come with our plans, our dreams, and our memories.

We come with our time, our gifts, and our skills.

We come with our family, our friends, and ourselves.

We come to offer to you everything we have and are.

We come to glorify your holy name. Amen.

2

AWARE OF YOUR HOLINESS

Lord, we come into your presence, aware of your holiness but drawn by your gentleness.

We come because we have heard of your mercy, and we come bringing our sinfulness.

We come confessing that you are Creator, aware of our need of your re-creation.

We come declaring your sovereignty and majesty and ready to offer thanksgiving and glory.

We come knowing that you are our judge but trusting your mercy and the grace of Christ.

We come because you are worthy of our worship and commitment; we come because you called us; we come because in you we have life, hope, and eternal life.

We come in Christ's name. Amen.

· 3 ·

IN A WORLD OF CHANGE

Lord, we live in a world of change.

Every day is filled with uncertainty.

We are surrounded by the twists and turns of life, and we often feel we have little or no control over things that happen to us.

Lord, we come to stand in your eternal presence.

We come to you to find ourselves, to find our way, to find hope.

We come to you because in Christ you first came to us. Amen.

· 4 ·

WE CALL YOU FRIEND

We call you friend, but your glory should overwhelm us.

We name you Lord, but we fail to recognize your sovereignty.

We sing your praises, but we do not reach into the heights of heaven.

We think of you as Father, but your kindness and love are beyond comparison.

We celebrate your truth and we acknowledge your glory, but our tiny, finite minds are hopelessly inadequate to comprehend your power.

Savior, Lord, Master, and King, we come with our imperfect lives and our impoverished praises.

Accept them in the name of Christ. Amen.

· 5 ·

COMING TO LISTEN

Lord, we have come to listen to you and to share with you all that is on our hearts and minds.

We have come to praise you and to give you thanks.

We have come because you are worthy and because of our need.

We have come because you are here and because you have promised to go with us when we leave.

Fill us with your love and empower us with your Spirit that we may worship you in Christ. Amen.

· 6 ·

WITH ANTICIPATION

Father, we come with a great sense of anticipation; we come expecting to meet you here.

We come, and we know that you will not disappoint us.

We come seeking your face, longing to give you praise and glory.

We have come that we might be made strong in Christ and be renewed by the power of your Holy Spirit. Amen.

· 7 ·

OUT OF THE DARKNESS

Father, when we come to you it is like walking out of darkness and into the light.

There are so many things, so many experiences that damage and spoil our lives each day.

There are so many things that prevent us from being the kind of people you meant us to be.

It would be so easy to come simply to be held in your healing, re-creating love.

Father, by your Holy Spirit enable us to be made whole by focusing on you and allowing your praise to be at the center of all we say and do today.

In the name of Christ, the one who makes all things new.
Amen.

· 8 ·

WE HAVE HEARD

Lord, we have heard of all that you have done in and through the lives of your people—through the centuries and across the world.

You have touched and changed humanity's whole way of living; you have made us new.

We have come to worship you, to be changed by you, to become the people you always meant us to be.

Let it happen, Lord, even though we are afraid of change and resist any alteration of our way of life.

Challenge us and change us and fill us with such an awareness of you and your presence that nothing, not even our own hearts and lives, can ever be the same again. Amen.

· 9 ·

YOU DESERVE PRAISE

Heaven and earth are full of your glory, almighty, eternal, most holy God.

You deserve the praise of every creature; you are worthy of worship and honor and love.

Creator, Sustainer, Redeemer, Renewer, perfect in wisdom and might, you reign supreme beyond time and space, in beauty and splendor and light.

We adore you, our God; we praise your great name; we offer you our worship through Jesus Christ, who because of his life, death, and resurrection is the center, the cause, and the object of our praise. Amen.

10

WE COME AS WE ARE

Lord, we come as we are that we may be changed by your grace.

We come with our emptiness that we may be filled.

We come with darkness, seeking your light.

We come with our weakness to receive your strength.

We come with our brokenness that you may make us whole, Lord.

We come as we are that we may be changed by your grace.

We come with our lives to be filled with your power.

We come with our worship to praise you forever.

We come with our words and our prayers, which we offer for your glory.

Lord, we come as we are that we may be changed by your grace. Amen.

· 11 ·

YOU KNOW, LORD

Lord, you know the hurt and anger we feel within us and the worries and concerns that are filling our minds.

You know our longing for our lives to be changed and for your love to heal our painful memories.

You know the things we have said and done and thought that have caused you pain and others heartache.

You know the emptiness we feel today and the anguish that still haunts and holds us.

You know the sorrow and doubt that all but overwhelms our lives.

You know that we do not find it easy to keep Christ at the center of our lives.

Open our eyes, Lord, so that we can see Jesus. Amen.

· 12 ·

YOUR PRESENCE CHANGES THINGS

Lord, your presence lifts us, your grace amazes us, your power overwhelms us, and your love excites us.

No matter what we bring with us—hurts, sorrows, self-satisfaction, bitterness, or joyful praise—you always receive us as we are and transform what we bring and fill us with gifts of your mercy. Amen.

· 13 ·

You Overwhelm Us

Lord, you overwhelm us.

Your might and majesty are beyond anything we can imagine or create.

Your glory is so great it simply cannot be contained.

Not even the vast expanse of time and space is sufficient to encompass your glory.

And yet—more wonderful still—you are here and you have come to receive our worship.

You have come to make your home even in our poor lives.

We have come to receive all that you are and all that you will give.

We have come in Jesus' name. Amen.

· 14 ·

The Good News

Lord, we have heard the good news of the life, death, and resurrection of your Son.

We have come now to experience its power, to hear your call, and to be sent out as disciples of Christ.

Lord, so fill our thoughts, our lives, and our lips with songs of praise that others will long to bring glory to him. Amen.

· 15 ·

Touch Our Lives

Lord, we do not find it easy to be open before you, and we often leave worship with the knowledge that while you were here, our minds and our thoughts were elsewhere.

Lord, we allow so many things to become obstacles between ourselves and you and your living presence.

Touch our lives with your love, and flood our worship with your Holy Spirit that we may offer Spirit-filled praise to you in Jesus' name. Amen.

16

THE FINGERPRINTS OF GOD

Lord, we praise you for the privilege of walking with Christ and bearing his name; for the joy that he has brought into our lives and the new sense of purpose we feel; for the meaning and direction he has given to our lives; for the peace, courage, and faith that he gives; for the laughter and love with which he has touched our days; and for the love that reaches out to fill us and transform our witness and worship and praise.

We praise you for Jesus and for the way he changes our lives.

We praise you that Jesus' story is true.

We praise you that it is not simply a story of events in the past but an experience of newness and renewal available to us through the Holy Spirit.

We praise you for those moments when the Spirit opens our eyes to the fingerprints of God in creation and our ears to his word in the Bible and to his voice in the presence of a friend.

We praise you for those times when we have known the touch of his love and have been used as channels of his caring. We praise you for the knowledge that his forgiveness has lifted our burden of guilt, his light has broken through our darkness, and his love is making us whole.

We praise you in the name of Christ, the one who makes all things new. Amen.

· 17 ·

EXTRAVAGANT LOVE

Almighty God, our heavenly Father, we praise you for your extravagant love that gives us hope, joy, and courage.

We praise you for your love that never lets us off, never lets us down, and never lets us go.

We praise you for your sovereignty and your holiness and that they are saturated in love.

We praise you for dealing with our fears, touching our lives, and healing our brokenness.

We praise you that in your wisdom and grace you did not leave us to try to find you in our own strength or to doubt the reality of your loving-kindness and mercy.

We praise you for always being there when we needed you most, for being there when we least expected it, for being with us when no one else could be there and no one else wanted to be there.

We praise you that every time we look to Christ we are reminded there is nothing he does not know about us and nothing he does not understand about our lives.

We praise you that you come to us again and again.

You lift us when we are down and hold us when we are hurting;

you fill us with your grace and share all the twists and turns of our lives.

Mighty God, wonderful Savior, living Lord, by your Holy Spirit enable us to give you the praise and glory you deserve. May the song we have begun ring out through all the world and to the end of time. Through Christ our Lord. Amen.

18

FAITH TO SHARE

Father, we praise you for the good news of Jesus Christ; for his life, death, and resurrection, which is the good news that sets us free to know you as Father, to live in hope, to be full of joy, and to be at peace.

We praise you that there is a story to tell, a message to proclaim.

We praise you that though we are often uncertain what to say to others about Christ and how to say it so that they will understand, we never need to be in any doubt that we have something to say and that it is true and worthy.

We praise you for the truth of the gospel and for the way it has touched, changed, and renewed people's lives through the centuries and continues to change lives today.

We praise you that in Christ we have proof of your love for each one of us and that there is no limit to what you can do in and through us.

We praise you for your determination to reconcile the whole world to yourself; that you were willing to pay the price to make this possible; and that it is now freely available for all.

We praise you for every time the gospel is preached and made known and for every person whose words and deeds make it real.

We praise you for baptism and holy communion, the sacraments that are pictures of your grace and truth.

Father, we praise you for all you have done for us and for the ways you use us as channels of your love.

We ask that, by your Holy Spirit, we may be equipped and empowered to make known the love of God and the grace of the Lord Jesus Christ.

We ask this in the name of him who died and was raised for all. Amen.

· 19 ·

GOD'S GREATNESS, OUR SMALLNESS

Lord, you do not change; you are always there, and you always will be.

We praise you for your greatness, which holds our smallness; for your majesty, which was once clothed with our humanity; for your sovereignty, which embraces our frailty; for your holiness, which exposes our sinfulness; for your wholeness, which heals our brokenness; for your glory, which fills our emptiness; for your love, which gives us life; for your Son, who claims us for his own; for your Spirit, who empowers us for worship, witness, and service.

Lord of all time and space and all things, we praise you that in Christ you came and shared all that life means to us so that we, by your grace, might enter into all that heaven is with you.

We have come to praise you for the coming of Christ our Savior and the Savior of the world.

In his name. Amen.

· 20 ·
GRACE FOR THE LOST

Lord, we praise you for your creative love and the compassion that all but overwhelms us.

We praise you for your love that was the source of all creation and for your grace that is forever seeking the lost, the broken, the defeated, and the forgotten.

We praise you for the way your mercy clothes your justice, and your forgiveness cleanses our sinful, selfish lives.

We praise you for your love that we have met in the life of Jesus Christ and for your truth that gives us solid hope.

We praise you not only that Jesus lived our life and entered into our earthly pain, but also that through his death and resurrection he has assured us that the past has already been dealt with and the future is safe in your hands.

We praise you for the coming of the Holy Spirit, who holds our lives and transforms our attitudes.

We praise you for the way you fill our minds with your word and our lives with your service.

We praise you that, though your majesty, glory, and authority mean that it will never be possible to know you completely in this life, the mystery of your sovereignty will always inspire us to worship you.

We praise you that in Christ you have revealed enough of your love and holiness, your grace and your authority, to enable us to know you as Savior and call you Lord.

We bring our praise in the name of Christ, sovereign Lord of all things forever. Amen.

· 21 ·

GLORY BEYOND WORDS

Lord, we praise you for the way you far exceed the limits of our minds.

Your mercy takes our breath away and your love knows no bounds.

We praise you for your glory, which is utterly beyond our imagining and for your goodness, which sustains the whole universe.

We praise you for your majesty, which leaves us speechless and your sovereignty, which gives us courage.

We praise you that you are not simply one god among many but that you are the one and only true and living God.

We praise you because you are the one who had no beginning, and we worship you because you have no end.

Your power stretches from one end of eternity to the other.

Before the world was made, before there was anything to be seen, before a sound was heard or a color excited the senses, you were God.

Before an idea was given shape, before a thought was set in motion, before time began, you were God.

Before there were seas and oceans, mountains and valleys, streams and rivers, plants and animals, before we came to be, you were God. Always and forever God, and we praise you.

We praise you for creating us in your image and giving us the desire to create and the ability to think, to plan, to choose, and to love.

Wonderful God! We praise you for your love showered over the whole of your creation and made flesh in Jesus Christ who came, lived, died, and was raised to life as a sign of your love.

We praise you that your love has reached out to our own hearts and lives and, through your Holy Spirit, is changing us and making us into the people you always meant us to be.

We praise you, and in Christ we give you all the glory. Amen.

THE APPEARANCES OF CHRIST

Lord, we praise you because you have shown us that you are not a dead hero to be honored and respected, who cannot share our lives today.

We praise you not only because you died to be our Savior but also because you rose again to be our Lord, that you were not only raised from the dead but also you are alive and present with us and you are our living Lord.

We praise you for the sense of peace, hope, joy, and meaning with which your presence fills our lives.

Lord, without you we would be lost, alone, and without hope.

Without your presence in our midst our worship would be empty, our Christian lives a meaningless experience, and our witness and service a pointless sham.

We praise you for your appearances to your disciples in their ordinary moments of life and in their everyday lives.

We praise you too for the way you have come to men and women through the centuries and that you have come into our lives too.

Lord, because you are alive and in the midst of all we say and do and are, you enable us to declare the good news with joy and hope and to do it for your glory. Amen.

23

THE PROMISE OF FREEDOM

Lord, you are far, far more wonderful than our words can ever say or our minds imagine.

We praise you because you are the source of all that is good and true and free.

It is your desire to fill our lives, our thoughts, and our hearts with all your goodness, truth, and love.

We praise you that you are a God who longs to set all your creatures free—free, not to please ourselves or make our own selfish plans or seek our individual personal satisfaction, but free to be the people you always meant us to be from the very beginning.

Lord, your offer of freedom begins with an empty cross, an empty tomb, and the "emptying out" of the Holy Spirit.

In the life, death, and resurrection of Christ, you have demonstrated your power to set all things free.

We praise you for the promise that we shall be with him, that in him we shall have all the resources of heaven and earth to enable us to praise you as you deserve.

Lord, may the freedom you give us in Christ bring you endless glory.

In the name of Christ, the one who sets us free. Amen.

· 24 ·

GOD'S WORD IN SCRIPTURE

Lord, we praise you, the living God.

We praise you, the God who is alive and the God who gives us life.

We praise you for your acts on behalf of your people through the centuries and across the world, for the record of all you have said and done in the Scriptures, for all we can learn of you through the work of the Holy Spirit upon the pages of the Bible.

We praise you for the truth we have received about Jesus Christ and his knowledge and love of the Scriptures, for the way they guided his life and ministry as your uniquely precious Son.

We praise you more that he has become the very focal point for every part of our lives and for the fulfillment of Scripture in him.

In his life on earth, his death on the cross, and his resurrection from the dead, he gathered up and completed all that, through the centuries, you had promised.

We praise you for the assurance in him that no matter the trials and problems we face today, we, like him, will share in your promise of the ultimate victory of your purposes for all your creation.

In the name of him whose life and presence fulfills your word. Amen.

· 25 ·

THE ONE WHO CHANGES THINGS

Lord, we praise you for the way you can take the ordinary things and make them new; you are able to take ordinary lives, lived by ordinary people, and fill them with meaning.

We praise you for your promise of joy and your offer of peace that can utterly transform how we live and respond.

We praise you for Jesus, who walked a hard path through his life, for the way he shared in the hopes and the fears of those around him, for the way he makes us aware of the demands of your love, and for the way that his presence still breaks hardened hearts.

We praise you for the way Christ touches and changes the whole of life.

He opens our eyes to the wonder of your creation and our ears to the songs of your love.

He opens our lips to praise you for his coming, living, dying, and rising.

He opens our hearts to receive him and to be filled with his life-transforming Spirit.

Lord, there is no God like you, no God besides you.

You are Lord of the whole of creation.

The universe is not large enough to contain the praise we want to offer you.

We praise you for Christ, the door and the key to new life, new beginning, and wholeness forever.

In his name and for his glory. Amen.

· 26 ··

GOD'S TRANSFORMING LOVE

Lord, we praise you, the one true living God, who fills the whole universe with life, love, and meaning.

We praise you for your tremendous love, which flows to us and into our lives in Christ.

Lord, it is your love that takes the people we are and makes it possible for us to be transformed into the people we are meant to be.

We praise you for your love, which sets us free from everything that holds us, from everything that squeezes real life out of us, and which brings us out of darkness into the glorious light of the Father's presence.

We praise you for reaching out for us and welcoming us home and for making us your sons and daughters; for the rest, refreshment, and hope with which you promise to fill our lives; for the assurance that we will share in the joyful celebration of your creative love and fill the universe with your glory.

We praise you here; we praise you now; we will praise you everywhere we go, as long as we live.

We will praise you eternally in ever increasing joy and worship with Jesus Christ our Lord. Amen.

· 27 ·

GOD'S SOVEREIGNTY

Father, you are greater than anything we can imagine, more wonderful than our deepest joy, more powerful than anything we have known.

Yours is the authority that always intended to create.

Yours is the sovereignty that holds all things in the palm of your hand.

Yours is the love that continually seeks to bring everyone, everywhere, into the joy of perfect fellowship with you.

Father, we adore you; we have come to lay our lives before you as we declare we love you, our God.

Father, we praise you for the demonstration of your authority, sovereignty, and love in the life, death, and resurrection of your Son, Jesus Christ our Lord. Amen.

· 28 ·

THE FOCAL POINT OF FAITH

Lord, we praise you for Jesus Christ, your Son and our Savior and our Lord.

We praise you that our faith is not just a matter of words; nor is it simply a question of being religious or sharing in the rituals of worship.

Christ himself is the focal point of all we say, do, and believe.

We praise you that he is the door, not only into life that is real but also to life eternal and to heaven itself.

We praise you that in Jesus we see your face.

In him we are confronted with your demand for obedience and trust.

Through him we receive all the love and the power at his disposal.

Father, in Christ we see all your glory compressed into one human life.

It is through him that we find our way to you, or rather, we are found by you.

Lord, almighty in your loving, all-knowing in your grace, overwhelming in your power—we are not afraid in your presence.

Gracious, loving Father, we find our greatest joy in praising you.

By your grace coming to us in Christ, enable us to begin a song of praise that flows from this place and brings you glory everywhere, every day, and forever. Amen.

· 29 ·

GOD EVER NEAR, EVER APPROACHABLE

Father, we praise you that whoever we are and wherever we go you are there.

We have discovered that there is simply nowhere we can go where you will not be present.

We cannot hide, we cannot run, we cannot even be at our destination before you!

You are always ahead of us, preparing the way.

You are there waiting with arms of love and mercy to hold us and to welcome us, to heal us and to hold us.

Lord, you are ever near, ever approachable.

In the midst of our anxiety and fear you are always understanding, coming into our turmoil, our doubts, our weakness, and despair; and you come with peace.

You stand guard over our hearts and minds so that we dare to speak your name and serve your kingdom.

Great and wonderful God, always loving, we praise and honor you.

Your majesty is beyond our reach, your fatherly love, so gentle and accepting, is always near.

We praise you for your love and truth made known in the word of the prophets, in your Word made flesh in Jesus, in his dying and his rising.

We praise you here and will praise you everywhere.

We praise you now and will praise you forever. Amen.

· 30 ·

LOVE FOR A FALLEN WORLD

Father, we praise you that no matter the depth of our sin, your love can reach down and lift us up; no matter the hurt and pain we feel, your love holds us and heals us; no matter how far we wander from you and your will for our lives, your love still reaches out to find us and bring us home.

We praise you that your love far exceeds our guilt, that though, in Christ's death on the cross, you have made clear the enormity of our sin, you accept us as we are.

You never allow us to become satisfied with the lives we live and the things we say and do, but you are always seeking to lift us up and make us new and make us whole.

We praise you most for your utter determination that we should be free—free to choose, free to live, free to praise, and free to serve.

We praise you for the freedom that comes to us in Christ, our Savior and Lord. Amen.

Prayers of Thanksgiving

MADE IN THE IMAGE OF GOD

Lord, we thank you for the splendor with which you have filled all creation; for the immensity of the universe, which defies our understanding; and for the beauty of our world, which is greater than our words to describe it.

We thank you for scientists and all people of learning who, in seeking to unlock its mysteries, provide more reasons for giving you praise.

We praise you for the place you have given us in your creation.

Thank you for those who, through words and pictures, through music and writing, have added to the beauty of your wonderful world; thank you that we reflect your image when we desire to create that which is good.

Thank you for all who are transformed by the sight of beauty, the touch of love, the care of compassion, the challenge of your word, the assurance of forgiveness, and the presence of Christ.

Thank you, most of all, for the good news of the life, death, and resurrection of Jesus, and for those moments when you break into our lives all over again; for helping us to recognize the purpose of your love in the whole of your creation.

We bring our prayer in Jesus Christ our Lord. Amen.

· 32 ·

THE LOVE AND MERCY OF GOD

Father, we thank you that you have not left us alone, but you have sought us out and welcomed us home.

We praise you that in every part of life and in every corner of our lives, your holiness calls us to confess the height of your glory and the depth of our sin.

Your mercy challenges us to trust you and empowers us to begin again.

We thank you that you have so designed our lives that we can know you and experience your presence, that you have created the world in such a way that everywhere we look, we can see your fingerprints.

We are grateful for each person whose words and deeds, and whose life and example, have spoken to us of you.

We thank you most of all for Jesus Christ, through whom you have made yourself known and knowable; that he lived our life, shared our pain, and overcame our death; that through your Spirit we can begin to know something of your life, love, and joy within us.

We thank you that we can enter each day and every situation, and that we can face all that life brings us, in the knowledge of your loving, caring, sovereign will.

In Jesus' name. Amen.

33

THE JOURNEY OF LIFE

Father, we thank you for the joy of life and for the wonderful world in which you have placed us; for all those whom you have given us to share our journey through life—for colleagues at work, for friends at church or at school, for those with whom we have shared precious moments, and for those who were there when we needed them.

We thank you for laughter and for tears, for seeing and for listening, for thinking and doing, and for just being alive.

Father, we thank you for the words and deeds of those who have changed life for other people; those who have brought the word of hope to those who are broken, the message of love to those who are down; those who have spoken words of forgiveness to those who were wrong, and whose lives have brought encouragement to those without joy.

Thank you for those who warn others of danger and those who declare the good news of Christ.

Father, we thank you for the whole life and ministry of Jesus which gives us hope and for the promise of the Holy Spirit, who gives us new life.

We bring our thanks in Christ's name. Amen.

34

CONFIDENCE IN CHRIST

Wonderful God! We thank you that you fill our hearts with your hope and our lives with a sense of expectation, that you heal our wounds and wipe away our tears, that you excite us with your grace and overwhelm us with your mercy, that in Christ's life, death, and resurrection you have demonstrated your victory over death and despair and given us the assurance that nothing, but nothing, can bring an end to your loving-kindness toward us or separate us from your love.

Thank you that you bring us through every time of pain, brokenness, and anxiety, that we can speak to others of your love in total confidence of its reality and its power to make all things new.

Thank you for the peace, hope, joy, and courage with which you have filled our lives and for the gratitude with which you have flooded our hearts.

Wonderful God!

We thank you and we praise you and we worship you, for you alone are worthy.

We ask that, by the Holy Spirit, you will take all that we have brought—our hymns, our words, and our prayers—and transform them through his powerful presence into joyful celebration that is worthy of the King of Kings and the Lord of Lords.

In the name of Christ the Lord. Amen.

35

THOSE IN POSITIONS OF LEADERSHIP

Father, we thank you for your sovereignty over all your creation and for your authority over the whole of our lives.

Thank you for those whose exercise of power and authority is for the good of those they seek to serve yet not for their own glory, for those whose wise and gentle leadership reflects your gracious kindness to us all in Christ, for parents whose loving discipline of their children provides a pattern for the whole of their lives and a contentment and understanding that will lead to maturity.

We thank you for all world leaders and those in positions of authority in the life of the nation—for those in the police force, the armed forces, for prison officers, probation officers, for judges and all those in the legal professions—who honor your name and give you the glory.

We thank you for those who know you and for those who do not but whose words and deeds reflect something of your love and compassion.

Thank you that when human authority is used for the good of all, it is simply an echo of your sovereign will and your loving authority.

We thank you that your authority is over all things and all people, and will last for all time, when time is no more.

In the name of him who is the Lord. Amen.

36

THE LIFE OF THE FAMILY

Lord, we thank you that you designed our lives to reflect your love, care, and compassion, for the sense of completeness that you bring to our lives, and for the realization that dawns upon us that without you there is no life that is real.

You are the source of all that is good and true and wholesome in the life of our families.

We thank you for the strength you give when times are hard and for the encouragement when we are facing times of distress and despair.

We thank you for those who support us through good times and bad and for those who remain faithful to each other no matter the cost.

We praise you for sharing our sadness and our sorrow and for understanding us when we are at the point of breaking.

We thank you most of all for Jesus and that through our faith in his life, death, and resurrection you have freely given us our place in the family of God.

Lord, we praise you that we belong to a family that knows no barriers and rejects all divisions.

We ask that you will fill us with the joy and the sense of anticipation of being members of your family with whom we will worship you for all eternity.

In the name of Christ. Amen.

· 37 ·

OUR HOPE IN CHRIST

Lord, we come to thank you for who you are and what you have done, that in Christ you lift us when we are down, you heal us when we are hurting, you hold us when we are broken, and you strengthen us when we are weak.

We thank you for your love, which will never be defeated and for your purposes, which will never end.

We praise you that you enrich our victories and you share in the pain of our defeats; that you cleanse us when we are sinful and restore us when we slip and fall; that you are with us when the pressures and strains of life seem to have no ending and the darkness of the world and our lives needs to be conquered by the light of Christ's love.

We thank you that you are strength for us when our strength fails, you are hope for us in our anguish and despair, you are grace for us when we have triumphed, and you are courage for us when we are afraid.

In the name of Christ, we bless your name. Amen.

· 38 ·

THE FELLOWSHIP OF GOD'S PEOPLE

Father, we praise you for the bundle of experiences we call life.

We thank you that you never intended us to journey through life in isolation.

You created us to be open to you and to each other.

From the first it was your intention that we should live in trust and fellowship with each other.

We know you have planted within us a restlessness that will not be satisfied by our selfish greed and our arrogant individualism.

We are aware of our sense of corporate dependence and our need of you and of each other.

We thank you that in Jesus we have been reconciled to you.

Through his life, death, and resurrection you have given us the good news. Barriers between us can be removed and our walls of division can be broken down.

We are filled with joy for every person who, through their words and deeds, through who they are and how they live, declares the good news of your healing love.

We ask that by your Holy Spirit you will so heal the disunity of Christ's body that our oneness in him and our fellowship with each other may bring honor and glory to your name and make known the reconciling love of Christ. Amen.

· 39 ·

CHRIST THE GOOD SHEPHERD

Father, we thank you for your love for all your creation, for your love ever reaching out to a lost and fallen world.

We thank you for your love unending, for your love made human in Jesus.

We praise you for your love incarnate—calling, searching, holding, risking everything in dying and rising.

We thank you for Christ, the Good Shepherd, who demonstrates the reality and power of your love.

We praise you for all that you accomplished in his life, death, and resurrection and that he is the door to hope and fulfillment, to peace and joy.

We thank you that in him there is freedom from fear and freedom to live, freedom to love and freedom to give, freedom to come and freedom to go, freedom to thank and freedom to trust, freedom to love and freedom to care, freedom to stand firm and freedom for all.

We thank you for those whose lives and words and deeds have made the love of Christ real for us, for those who have stood by us, for those who have tried to understand, and for those who have loved us no matter the cost.

Father, our Father, we thank you and ask that we may be shepherds in your name.

For Christ's sake. Amen.

· 40 ·

SEEKING THE LOST

Father, our Father, we rejoice that you have filled us with the spirit of thankfulness and praise; that although you know us utterly and completely, you still love us and welcome us into the joy of your presence; that though we often leave the path and wander off on our own, you are still there with arms of love and mercy to welcome us home.

We thank you that we do not have to go in search of you, because you are the God who comes looking for us; that you call us to be friends of Jesus and the sons and daughters of your love.

We thank you for your extravagant love that goes on forgiving again and again; that every time we look at the cross of Christ we know that though there are times when we sink very low, your Son, as a sign of your love, sank even lower.

We are filled with gratitude that he is the sign of the lengths to which you are prepared to go to deal with our sin, to heal our wounds, and to restore our hope.

Heal us, Father, and bring us home.

For Christ's sake. Amen.

· 41 ·

OVERCOMING TEMPTATION

Father, we thank you for your Son, Jesus Christ, who faced all the temptations that come to us all.

We thank you more for the assurance that in him temptation can be defeated; that we can live victorious lives for him and through him.

We praise you for those who have remained faithful to what they know to be true even at the cost of the support of family and friends, for those who have faced all kinds of pressure and persecution for their faith in Christ and refused to deny him as their Savior and Lord, for those who have stood against injustice and oppression, and for those who have faced deep disappointment and great frustration but have preferred to walk with Christ rather than with the crowd.

We thank you for the assurance that in the cross of Christ and in his resurrection we can overcome all our trials and temptations through him who has won the victory. Amen.

· 42 ·

CELEBRATION AND JOY

For the world in which you have placed us, for the people with whom we share our daily experiences of life,

We thank the Lord.

And we celebrate with joy!

For those who provide for our needs and comfort us in our despair, for those who lift us when we are down, who accept us as we are, and who forgive us even when we are wrong,

We thank the Lord.

And we celebrate with joy!

For those whose words and deeds make the love of God real for us, for those whose lifestyle is so shaped by the presence of the Father that they are beacons of hope in a dark, dark world,

We thank the Lord.

And we celebrate with joy!

For those who have borne witness to the one who lived, died, and was raised to make us whole, for those who told us the stories of Jesus, for those who brought us to Christ,

We thank the Lord.

And we celebrate with joy!

For those whose warmed hearts have revealed the renewing and enabling power of the Holy Spirit, for those lives that demonstrate the fruit and the gifts of the Spirit's presence,

We thank the Lord.

And we celebrate with joy!

For the servants of God whose vision has brought us to this time and place, for those who through the years have stood firm for Christ, for those who have finished the race and won the prize,

We thank the Lord.

And we celebrate with joy!

For our life in Christ and the fellowship of his people, for freedom to worship and good news to share, for opportunities for evangelism and the mission of caring,

We thank the Lord.

And we celebrate with joy!

For our gathering together in the name of Christ, for our oneness in him and the promise of wholeness both now and to come, for the God who had the first word and assures us that he will have the last, for the one who is worthy,

We thank the Lord.

And we celebrate with joy! Amen.

· 43 ·

GOD'S SPECIAL POSSESSION

Father, we thank you not simply for making us but for giving us life, for the sheer joy of being alive, for the pleasure of real friendship, and for the opportunities to enjoy your wonderful creation.

We praise you that because of your hand in our creation we can find renewal and satisfaction and a sense of completeness not only in the world around us but also in the love with which you have filled our lives.

We thank you not only for making us but for making us your special people.

You have done this not because we are worthy but because we must bear a special responsibility.

Thank you for giving us a world to care for, for surrounding us with people whose needs are our opportunities to show your love and kindness, for helping us to see even the times of difficulty as opportunities to rediscover your strength and power.

We praise you for the faith with which you have filled our lives, for the growing certainty that you will never fail us, for your peace, love, and mercy, which are the things that really matter.

Thank you for Jesus Christ, through whom we are made your special possession. Amen.

· 44 ·

THE PROMISE OF FORGIVENESS

Father, we thank you for being ready to forgive us whenever we turn to you and honestly acknowledge your power and our own need.

We praise you for the joy of knowing that no matter who we are or what we have done or failed to do, we can experience the joy of forgiveness and beginning again.

Father, we thank you for the fellowship of your church, the community of those who have confessed their sin and are receiving your promise of life made whole.

Thank you for those who share your love with us and for those who demonstrate the reality of Jesus' love in all they say and do, for those whose offer of forgiveness has set us free to begin again and has been a sign to us of your love, which is always reaching out to us in Christ.

We bring our thanks in the name of Christ, the true source of all thankfulness. Amen.

· 45 ·

LIVING THE LIFE OF FAITH

Father, we thank you for those whose labors enrich our lives and for those whose words and deeds make our lives worthwhile, for those who care for your world and for those who seek to repair the damage we have done to your good earth.

Thank you for artists and writers, poets and painters, composers and musicians, and for all craftsmen and women who use their skills and their talents to display the beauty of your creation.

Thank you for the signs and reflections of your goodness and love in the lives of those you have touched with your grace, for those who risk their lives for the safety of others, for those who sacrifice everything to bring others the joy and the hope and the love of Christ.

We thank you for Christ and for his life, death, and resurrection and for his living presence with us now and always.

Lord, fill us with such an overflowing abundance of your Holy Spirit that we may be enabled to offer you the whole of our lives as a thank offering to your praise and glory.

In the name of Christ who makes us whole. Amen.

Prayers of Confession

· 46 ·

STRENGTH TO BEGIN AGAIN

Lord, we thank you for the love and power and mercy that have brought us to this moment in our lives and our life together.

We confess that we have not always wanted the best for each other or for those around us.

We confess that we have too often and too easily pleased ourselves and put our own wants and needs before those of others.

We confess that we have memories of the past that still hurt us, that we do not always find it easy to cope with what is happening today, and that tomorrow's uncertainty sometimes makes us afraid.

Lord, we ask not only for forgiveness but for the desire and strength to begin again. Amen.

· 47 ·

FEELING UNWORTHY

Father, we confess that we have often felt as Moses must have felt when he experienced your holy presence.

We confess that we are aware of moments of feeling utterly unworthy of you and your grace.

We confess that we have often known times when we have been ashamed and afraid of your coming too close to us.

We confess that we feel unclean whenever you are near and that we feel utterly inadequate to do justice to your glory.

We confess the mess we have made and continue to make of our lives.

We confess that though we call ourselves Christians and have opened our lives to Christ and have been filled with the Holy Spirit, we often feel that we are not greatly different from those who do not know you.

Lord, touch us, hold us, cleanse us, forgive us, and renew us.

And do it for your glory. Amen.

48

THE GOD WHO KNOWS US

Father, you know who and what we are and what we are not.

You know our confusion and our falling.

You know our strengths and our shame.

You know our professions of hope and just how quickly we lose heart.

You know our failure to stand firm on the faith we proclaim and our criticism of others who fail.

You know our complaints when we suffer and our refusal to share each other's hurts.

You know our self-satisfaction, our self-interest, and our selfishness.

You know of the conflict between our good intentions and our love of the easy way forward.

You know the battles we failed to win because we were never quite sure just whose side we were on.

Forgive us that we lose the struggle so easily because we insist on standing in our own strength and not in our Lord's.

Forgive us, restore us, and reclaim us as your own, through Christ. Amen.

· 49 ·

OUR FAILURE TO LOVE

Father, forgive us for every failure to love our neighbor as ourselves; forgive every thoughtless word, every selfish thought, and every unkind deed; forgive all our refusals to be open to your Spirit and to allow him to make our lives new; forgive us for our failure to enter into the victory of Christ by our refusal to carry the cross.

Father, open our eyes, our ears, our hearts, and our minds, and by your grace make us into the people you meant us to be from the very beginning.

We ask this not only for our own benefit but for your glory. Amen.

· 50 ·

WHEN WE ARE DEAF

Lord, you speak, but we are deaf.

You call, but we do not want to listen.

You challenge us, but we close our ears.

You hold out your hand to guide and to lift us, but we turn away from you.

You reach out to give us your comfort, but we are too self-confident to receive it.

You join us on our journey, but we do not recognize you.

You try to change the direction of our lives, but we think that we know best.

You warm our cold hearts, you inspire our faith, and you forgive us again and again, and we are amazed.

Lord, open our hearts to your grace and renew our hope and faith in Christ our Lord. Amen.

· 51 ·

ISOLATION

Lord, we confess that each of us has known times when we have felt alone, empty, and abandoned.

We have experienced a sense of isolation from you and those around us.

We confess that we easily become anxious about ourselves, our families, our health, and our possessions.

We confess that we are too easily brought low by our concerns and by our reliance on the false security of earthly things, and we do not stand on the rock you have provided.

Lord, set our feet again on the path of life where you would have us walk.

Keep our eyes fixed on Christ, the source of new life, and by your Spirit give us your truth, which sets us free.

In Christ's name. Amen.

52

OUR DISUNITY

Father, forgive us for the disunity of your church and the brokenness of Christ's body.

Forgive us for the way we allow our words and deeds to destroy hope and diminish other people's lives.

Forgive us for our selfish, arrogant criticism of others and our failure to be the meek of the earth.

Forgive us that too often we reflect the attitudes and values of a world that has turned its back on its Maker and not those of the kingdom of God.

Forgive us that we break what was meant to be whole and hinder everything that would bring healing and trust.

Forgive us, renew us, and make us vessels of grace to a broken, hurting world. Amen.

53

SHUTTING OUT GOD

Father, we confess that we have not listened for your voice and have allowed the clamor of the world and the busyness of our lives to drown your words of warning and challenge.

We confess that we have closed our eyes to the signs of your presence and activity in the world.

We have closed our ears to your call to share our plenty with the poor, the hungry, and the starving.

We have made no time to be still and know that you are God.

We have been too busy to read your word and to pray.

We have been careless when you called us to be careful.

We have been selfish when you required us to give.

We have been hard-hearted when you longed for us to be gentle and understanding.

We have been resistant to change when you wanted to make all things new.

We have neglected opportunities to serve in your name, to visit the sick, to give a cup of water in your name, and to tell someone else of your love for us.

Father, we are ashamed, and we know that we have not been living as true citizens of your kingdom.

Forgive our indifference, our selfishness, and our disobedience. Touch our hearts, change our attitudes, and make our lives new. For Christ's sake. Amen.

54

TAKING ADVANTAGE

Father, forgive us for the way we take advantage of each other and seek our own benefit at each other's expense.

Forgive us for those who are discouraged because of what we have said and done and for those who are hurting because we failed to help and to care.

Forgive us for accepting the standards of a world that has turned its back on its Maker.

Forgive us that we measure the importance of things by their monetary value and that our measure of truth is determined by convenience.

Forgive us for accepting the falsehoods of those around us and for assuming there is no right and wrong.

Forgive us for not standing more firmly for your truth and for being so aggressive and insensitive when we do.

Forgive us for accepting that life is a lottery, where we win because others have lost and we succeed because others have failed.

Lord, fill us with your gentle, healing, compassionate Spirit, and give us your wisdom in all things.

By your Holy Spirit enable us to live the life of faith in hope, joy, and love, and may we love our neighbor as ourselves and give you all the praise and glory. Amen.

· 55 ·

THE WORDS WE USE

Father, we are full of words, but they are often words of anger, bitterness, and jealousy.

We use our words to hurt others, to spoil relationships, and to build barriers between us.

We use words to make ourselves sound compassionate, but our thoughts are selfish and our intentions self-centered.

We use words to criticize others, to belittle and to gossip, hurting you and our neighbor.

We have no right to ask for forgiveness and there is no earthly reason why you should cleanse and renew us.

We simply have faith that in Christ you will.

Father, speak the word of hope, of mercy, of cleansing and renewal, and give us the power and compassion to offer them to each other.

In the name of Christ, whose name is love. Amen.

· 56 ·

OUR ADDICTIONS

Father, we confess that we often take life for granted.

We allow our days to slip by without offering you a word of thanks and praise for the time we have been given.

Father, we confess that we enjoy sitting in judgment on the faults and failings of others but turn a blind eye to our own.

We confess our love of other people's praises and our addictions to their compliments.

We confess our failure to acknowledge our own weaknesses and the hurt we cause you and each other.

We confess our enjoyment of gossip and our lack of love for our neighbor, because we have never been able to accept ourselves.

Lord, forgive us, cleanse us, and renew us.

Fill us all over again with your love.

Heal our hearts, our minds, and our lives.

Do this not for our sakes alone but that we might become channels of your healing for our neighbor and your world. Amen.

· 57 ·

OUR EASY EXCUSES

Lord, we are full of excuses when we should bring confession.

We are ready with questions, though you are the answer.

We seek ways to easily avoid our commitment, but you have given us responsibilities we cannot escape.

We confess that we have often remained silent when you called us to speak; that we have done nothing when you required us to act.

Forgive us when we try to make everything as complicated as we can, hoping to avoid your answer.

Forgive us for turning our back on our neighbor in the pretence we were too busy and we thought you might not notice.

Father, forgive us, change us, and make even our lives and our lips signs of your hope and channels of your miracle of grace to a lost and hurting world. Amen.

58

TOO BUSY

Father, forgive us that we fill our minds with many things that cause us hurt and confusion instead of focusing our attention on Christ.

We confess that we make space in our lives for the things we want to do, then we pretend we are too busy to serve you.

We confess that we are quick to criticize others and to judge them for the very same things of which we ourselves are guilty.

Forgive us our lack of sympathy, our failure to show mercy, and our neglect of compassion.

Forgive us for being pleased when other people make mistakes; their failures becoming known by everyone.

Forgive us our lack of sensitivity and understanding of each other's needs and fears.

Forgive us when we are unforgiving, and make us new and clean again.

Through Christ our Lord. Amen.

·59·

SELF-DECEPTION

Lord, forgive our harsh words and our unkind thoughts.

Forgive us for the way we deceive ourselves and one another.

Forgive us for the way we so gladly receive the love of Christ but are so slow to share it.

Forgive us that we rejoice in the freedom he makes possible but neglect your commission to bring others the good news that would open their prison too.

Forgive us that we allow our convictions to become prejudices and our assurance to become an excuse for not thinking through what we believe.

Forgive us for the way we enjoy putting others in the wrong and for our thoughtless criticisms of others that deny your love.

Forgive us, cleanse us, hold us again in your understanding arms, and give us courage to begin again. Amen.

60

KNOWN BY GOD

Lord, you know us better than we know ourselves.

You know our strengths and our weaknesses, our victories and our defeats, our pain and the hurt we cause each other.

You know we are not pure and clean when we stand before you, but when we confess our sin and affirm that Jesus is Lord, you clothe us in him and restore our relationship with you and with each other.

Forgive us our harsh words, our self-centeredness, and our over-confidence.

Forgive us our failure to trust you in everything.

Forgive us our insensitivity to the needs of others and our excuses when we go wrong.

Teach us your truth, fill us with your grace, and by your Holy Spirit empower us to love one another as Christ has loved us. Amen.

Prayers of Worship

THE LOVE OF JESUS

Father, we praise you for Jesus.

Thank you for the way he trusted you.

Thank you that he was so certain of your love.

We praise you that he trusted you all the way to the cross to become our Savior.

Thank you for the promise that we can share his resurrection life and power.

Father, we thank you that Jesus is not just a name in the Bible but our living Lord.

We praise you that he is not a long-dead hero but a friend for us today.

Thank you that he can be trusted and will share everything we face.

Thank you that he is always with us, not simply when we are together in church.

Thank you that he is with us at home, at school, at work, and in the world.

Thank you that he is there when we play games and when we are working very hard; that he is with us when things are going well and when everything seems to be going wrong.

Thank you that he is with us when we are strong and when we are weak, when we are good and when we are not.

Thank you that he is with us when we are fit and healthy, and when we are ill and in great need.

Thank you that he is with us when he is most needed and when we least expect him to be there.

Thank you that he is with us when we are kind and understanding, and when we want our own way and deliberately choose what we know is wrong.

Thank you for your forgiveness. Please make our lives new.

We ask this in Jesus' name. Amen.

62

WHAT WE CAN DO AND WHAT WE CAN BE

Lord, we have come to praise you for life and all the good things of life.

We thank you for the world in which we live and for the variety of colors and shapes all around us.

Thank you that we have eyes to see and ears to enjoy it all.

We praise you for those who love us and those whom we are called to love.

Thank you for those who serve us and help us.

Thank you for sending us to offer love and care to our neighbor.

Thank you for those moments of joy, peace, and hope that flood into our hearts.

Thank you that you fill each day with new reasons to turn and give you thanks and praise.

Thank you for Jesus.

Thank you for his life on earth and for the things he said and did, pointing to your love for us all.

We praise you for his healing and help for those who came to him in great need.

We praise you for his victory over all that spoils life, and we thank you for the freedom he gives in our lives.

Thank you for the coming of the Holy Spirit to touch and change our lives.

Thank you that he empowers us for worship and gives us the courage to tell others about you.

We are sorry, Lord, because we know that we have said and done things that have hurt you and spoiled life for others and ourselves.

Forgive us, not simply that we may feel better but that we may begin to live in the way that pleases you.

We ask this in the name of Jesus. Amen.

63

GOD WHO IS CHANGING US

We praise and thank you for loving us so much.

We thank you for your love to us in Jesus.

We thank you that he died to make us new.

We thank you for his resurrection and your promise to change us completely.

We praise you for all the gifts with which you fill our lives and for the joy we can have in using them for you.

We thank you for the gift of life and for those who share each day with us.

We thank you for those who share our hopes and our fears, our joys and our sorrows.

We thank you for the gift of family and friends, of games to play and things to learn.

We praise you for the gift of your creation and that we can see, hear, and enjoy everything good around us.

We thank you for helping us to love those who are unkind, to care for those who are lonely, and to forgive those who have hurt us most.

Forgive us for not trusting you enough and not allowing you to change our lives.

Forgive us for not forgiving those who have hurt us and let us down.

Through your love help us to begin again.

For Christ's sake. Amen.

· 64 ·

GOD'S PEOPLE

Father, we praise you for the life of your church and for the friendship and fellowship we share together.

We thank you that though we are all very different people who come from different places and speak many different languages, we are part of the one church of Jesus all over the world.

We are of different ages and we like different things; we have different ideas and we have different needs; but we have all put our trust in Jesus.

We praise you that though we think different things are important and we enjoy doing different things, it is our faith in Jesus that makes us one.

We thank you for making us members of your one family and for calling us by the name of your Son.

Though we are your family, we often still say and do the wrong things and we make mistakes, so we have to come to tell you that we are sorry.

But we are still your family, not because we are good enough, but because you have called us and chosen us and made us your own.

Father, forgive us for everything we say and do that damages the life of your church.

Forgive us for everything that breaks what should be whole.

Forgive us that so often we appear like those who do not know Jesus as their Savior; like those who do not call him Lord.

Forgive us, make us new, and make us one in Christ's name.
Amen.

65

God's Faithfulness

Heavenly Father, we praise you not only for making us but also
for your love and care.

We thank you that though we cannot see you, you have promised that you are always with us.

You have promised that no matter what we do, where we go, or
what we are facing, you will never leave us.

We praise you that wherever we look we can see the signs of
your presence with us.

We thank you for making yourself known in Jesus; that he
shares everything life means to us.

We thank you that he is like a shepherd; that he knows each
one of us by name and cares about each of us every day.

He is the one who will help us, guide us, lead us, and keep us safe.

We thank you for those who care for us when we are sick or in
hospital.

We thank you for family and friends whose love and kindness
make each day special.

We thank you for opportunities to help other people and to
show them your love and care.

Forgive us when we keep your love and care for ourselves and when we do not help others.

Forgive us for always wanting the biggest and the best of everything, for being greedy, selfish, and jealous.

By your Holy Spirit give us the strength we need to follow Jesus.

We ask this in his name. Amen.

· 66 ·

LIFE IS FOR LIVING

Father, we praise you that living in your world is so exciting.

We praise you for filling it with so many challenging things to do and so many exciting things to discover.

We thank you for the way you have made us.

We praise you for things we can do and learn.

We thank you that we can help other people know they matter, for the things we can say to make others feel welcome.

We thank you that Jesus shared our life; that he used his skill in his work as a carpenter.

We thank you for times when we are busy and times when we can rest, for times when we can offer help and care to others, and for times when we can be loved in return.

We thank you for the things we do at home, at school, at work, and in the wider world.

We thank you for games to play and times to laugh and have fun.

We praise you for the satisfaction of a job well done and for the good feelings we get from caring for those in need.

Forgive us when we are lazy and leave our work unfinished.

Forgive us when we work too hard and never stop and rest.

Forgive us for not making more space in our lives for you and for being too busy to read your word and to speak to you in prayer.

We ask this in the name of Jesus. Amen.

67

DAILY LIFE

Father, we praise you for the gifts and skills you have put into our lives.

We thank you that we have eyes to see, ears to hear, and minds to think.

We praise you for giving us a desire to learn more about you and your world.

We thank you for all those inventions that make life easier and safer: for cars and computers, cell phones and washing machines, wheelchairs and heart monitors.

We praise you for lives made more comfortable and for lives that have been saved, for the fun and excitement that modern technology has added to our lives.

Forgive us whenever we put our possessions before people, ourselves and our dreams before the needs of others.

Forgive us whenever we put anyone or anything before you.

Forgive us for pleasing ourselves and not listening to your call to love our neighbor.

Hear our prayer and fill us again with your love and joy. Amen.

68

LOVE THAT UNDERSTANDS

Father, we thank you that we can come to you just as we are.

We praise you that you know us completely.

We do not have to pretend; you know what we are really like.

We thank you that you still love us.

We praise you that in Jesus you shared all that this life means to us.

We thank you that through him we can enter the heaven of your love.

We are glad that you know the things that hurt us.

We thank you for understanding our fears.

We praise you that we never need to feel unloved, unwanted, or unnecessary.

We thank you for your promise to be with us always, and we praise you for the hope that Jesus makes possible.

Father, forgive us for not showing love to each other, for our failure to help those in need, for the foolishness that spoils our lives.

Forgive us, and fill us with the love of Jesus.

In his name. Amen.

· 69 ·

FOLLOWING JESUS

Lord, we praise you for your goodness, your power, and your glory.

We thank you for being so patient with us in our weakness and for understanding our doubts and fears.

We thank you for the ordinariness of Jesus' disciples and that being with him changed their lives.

We praise you that following him made their lives extraordinary.

We thank you that we are told about the disciples' strengths and weaknesses, their faith, and also their doubts.

We thank you for the questions they asked Jesus and his gentle response to their concerns.

We thank you for the call of Matthew, who had seemed more interested in money than in you;

James and John, who argued with everyone; and for Peter, who even denied he knew Jesus.

We thank you for Thomas, who was honest about his doubts and his fears but confessed you as Lord.

We thank you for all who have helped us to know you, those whose words and deeds have made you so real.

We are sorry that our lives and our worship make it harder for others to trust you.

We are sorry that we still rely on our own strength.

Please help us to speak of your love.

We bring our prayer in the name of our Lord. Amen.

70

THE GIFT OF TIME

Lord, you have given us so many things and you have given us so much love.

We thank you that you not only made the world but also go on making life new.

We thank you for food to eat and clothes to wear, for work to do and games to play, for things to learn and minds that can understand, for time on our own and time with our family and friends.

We thank you for Jesus, who was often busy but always had time for others.

He still made time to stop, to rest, to worship, and to pray.

We praise you that you did not make us to be like machines.

We thank you that you meant us to make time to relax, to play games, and to enjoy the fun of life.

We praise you that you told us to keep one day special for you and for ourselves.

You meant us to have one special day to remember you and your love and to give you praise.

We thank you that every Sunday we celebrate again Jesus' mighty resurrection.

Forgive us for not keeping Sunday special and for using your day just for ourselves.

Forgive us for our failure to make it a time to help, to care for, and to serve others.

Lord, forgive us and fill us with the peace of Jesus.

In his name. Amen.

· 71 ·

CONFLICT, TEMPTATION, AND FORGIVENESS

Lord, we praise you because you are the King of creation.

We thank you that there is no one and nothing greater than you.

You are greater than anyone who has ever lived, greater than anyone yet to be born, and greater than anyone living today.

We thank you because you made your world worth living in.

You planned this to be a place where we can find happiness, joy, and real life.

You always wanted everyone to feel loved, wanted, and of real value.

You meant everyone to live in freedom and without fear.

You made your world and filled it with hills and valleys, seas and oceans, streams and rivers, plants and animals, birds and insects, fish and fruit.

But you gave us the freedom to choose.

We have chosen to please ourselves and we have broken your laws.

We have spoiled your world as we have spoiled our lives.

Lord, we thank you that you loved us enough to send Jesus, and we praise you that he is the door to your kingdom.

We are sorry that we give in to temptation and that we find it so hard to stand firm for you.

Forgive us when we are weak, and help us because you are the King of the kingdom.

We ask this in Jesus' name. Amen.

· 72 ·

Standing Firm for Jesus

Father, we do not always find it easy to trust you or to follow Jesus Christ.

We do not always find it easy to know what we should say or do.

Even when we know what is right, we do not find it easy to do.

Father, we often feel we are poor examples for you and your kingdom.

We thank you for understanding just how hard it can be to follow Jesus and how easy it is to give in to what is wrong.

We praise you that we can know his strength, his encouragement, and his courage.

We thank you not only that Jesus lived our life and died on the cross but that he was raised to life again and is always with us.

He knows what it means to be let down by his friends and feel rejected.

We praise you for the promise of your Holy Spirit.

We thank you that he lives in our hearts and changes our lives.

We thank you for your promise that we will never stand by ourselves, but you will always stand with us.

Forgive us for those times when we have felt like giving up and giving in.

Forgive us when we have been ashamed of you and your love.

Forgive us and protect us and keep us safe in our walk with you.

We ask this in Jesus' name. Amen.

73

THOSE WHO CARE FOR OTHERS

Lord, we praise you for your wonderful world, and we thank you for the changing seasons.

We thank you for the life you have given to us and that every day we can enjoy all that you have made.

We thank you for all those who work to keep us safe and well, for policemen and women, for those who work in the fire service, for those who drive ambulances and those who work in hospitals, for dentists who care for our teeth, and for opticians who look after our eyes.

We thank you for pharmacies where we get our medicine, and for markets where we buy our food.

We thank you for those who keep our roads clean and for those who take away all our trash.

We thank you for all who add something special to our lives, and for those who show us the right way to live.

We thank you for Jesus, who showed us your love and that through his life, death, and resurrection he has opened the way for us to know you as our Friend, our Father, and our Lord.

Forgive us for forgetting to show your love to each other and for too often thinking only of ourselves.

Forgive us when we keep your love for ourselves and forget those who have no idea of their value to you.

Help us, by our words and deeds, to make your love known.

In the name of Jesus. Amen.

74

GOD MADE REAL

Father, we praise you because you are so great and so wonderful.

You are far, far greater than anything we can think of and far, far more wonderful than anything or anyone we have known.

We praise you that though Jesus taught us to call you our Father, you are a more loving father than any earthly father could ever be.

Jesus came so that we might learn how much you love us, but your love is more amazing than anything we have known.

You are not only full of glory and goodness, but your greatness is more than our minds can really understand.

In Jesus you showed us enough of who and what you are so that we can trust you with the whole of our lives.

We thank you for those who make us feel special and for those who give us encouragement, help, hope, and love.

We thank you for those who make us feel wanted and needed.

We thank you most of all for Jesus and his love for us all.

We praise you that he is the way to live, the truth about you, and the promise of real life to those who put their trust in him.

Forgive us when we try to live our lives our own way.

Forgive us for the mess we make of our own lives and for the way we hurt each other.

We ask that you will help us to begin all over again.

In Jesus' name. Amen.

· 75 ·

THE AMAZING LOVE OF JESUS

Lord, we praise you for your patience with us and that you care for us no matter what.

We praise you for your love that touches us when we are sad and holds us when we are afraid.

We thank you for those who stand by us, even when we make a mess of our lives.

We thank you for those who still love us, even when we let them down again and again.

We thank you for those who reach out to those who are lost and alone, to those who are homeless, and to those who cannot go home.

We thank you that each of us is special to Jesus and that he calls us to serve him by name.

Forgive us when we make excuses or try to blame someone else.

Forgive us when we do not listen for your call to serve you or for your challenge to trust you again.

Forgive us most of all where we are unforgiving, and make us new and clean again.

We ask this in the name of Jesus Christ our Lord. Amen.

Prayers of Intercession

LIFE-CHANGING POWER

We pray for the whole church of Jesus Christ.

We thank you for the message of hope, joy, peace, and heaven that you have given us in Christ.

May all your people be filled with confidence and with the certainty of their faith in Christ and in the power of self-giving love.

We pray that the people of God will have the knowledge of the dying and rising Christ and the power of the Spirit that will enable them to speak your truth with power.

The Lord hears our prayer.

Thanks be to God.

We pray for Christians everywhere: for those in positions of authority over others, for those with great responsibility in the life of the world, for politicians who are genuinely seeking to serve God and live by their faith in Christ, for those who take their faith into the boardrooms of industry, for those who still live for Christ in corridors of power, and for those who name his name in the face of ridicule and rejection.

May they know the strength and humility of Christ.

The Lord hears our prayer.

Thanks be to God.

We pray for Christians who are disillusioned: for those who made their commitment to Christ many years ago but who have slowly allowed their hearts to grow cold and their worship to become infrequent, for those who began with high hopes and determination to follow wherever Christ led but have allowed the world and its attitudes to write their agenda, for Christians whose faith is weak, for those whose knowledge of Christ has never grown, and for those who no longer pray or read God's word.

May they feel again the life-changing, life-renewing power of the Holy Spirit.

The Lord hears our prayer.

Thanks be to God.

We pray for Christians who are facing the onset of serious illness and for those caring for their loved ones, for those facing the certainty of loss, suffering, or death, for those who cannot let go of past failures, who have no peace today and are filled with fear for tomorrow, for those who are rediscovering the presence and power of the Spirit, for those in whose lives Christ is an inner spring welling up to life eternal.

The Lord hears our prayer.

Thanks be to God.

We pray for those whose faith sends them out to feed the hungry, to give with generosity, to love and comfort those who mourn; for those whose faith enables them to forgive those who have hurt them most and to become channels of hope to their hopeless, helpless neighbor; for ourselves, that however much it costs in pain or sorrow, in loving and understanding, we shall have the joy of winning others for Christ.

May the love of Jesus fill us, change us, and hold us.

The Lord hears our prayer.

Thanks be to God.

In the name of Christ, the source and power of our faith.

Amen.

77

FAMILIES

Father, we pray for our homes and for all our relationships there.

We ask that they will be surrounded by walls of love, care, and understanding.

We think of all those we know as brother or sister, father or mother, aunt or uncle, and those who have that title, for that is what they mean to us.

We pray, help us to show our gratitude to them for all they say and do.

We pray too for families and relationships that are under pressure, even to the point of breaking.

Help them to build walls of love and security.

Lord, in your mercy, hear our prayer.

Father, we pray, teach us and all families, including the family of the church, to know and love your will and your word.

We thank you that you have shown us how you intended us to live, speak, and behave; that in Jesus Christ, and through the Scriptures, we can have no excuse for not knowing how you meant us to live.

We pray, help all families to be ready to read your word and obey it and to seek to live for you in a world that has turned its back on its Maker.

We pray for families where there is worry, fear, bitterness, disobedience, or unfaithfulness.

Lord, in your mercy, hear our prayer.

Father, we pray that you will teach our family and all families to begin to think less about themselves and more about the world for which Christ died.

We pray for our own family, the family of the church, and the family of the human race.

May we seek opportunities of love and service, of caring and concern for others, that we may be open to every opportunity you provide to serve, care for, help, and love those in need.

Lord, in your mercy, hear our prayer.

In the name of Christ. Amen.

THE HOUSE OF GOD

We pray for the whole church of Jesus Christ throughout the world.

It worships, serves, and cares in different ways and in different places and through very different people.

Let us ask God to remind us that we are one in Christ.

The Lord hears our prayer.

Thanks be to God.

We pray for churches that are trapped in old buildings inherited from a previous generation, which have long since outlived their usefulness and have become a burden to today's congregations.

Let us ask God to open the doors of hope and new vision.

The Lord hears our prayer.

Thanks be to God.

We pray for congregations that are locked up in their churches, for those that are content to meet for their private worship behind closed doors every Sunday with little or no thought for the millions outside.

Let us ask God for the wind of the Spirit for renewal and mission.

The Lord hears our prayer.

Thanks be to God.

We pray for churches whose worship is faithful but locked up in the words they have always used, for those whose hearts and minds are closed to new patterns of worship and presenting the old gospel in words and ways that reach many more people.

Let us ask God for the courage to embrace all that is good in the new, and for the wisdom to save what is good from the past.

The Lord hears our prayer.

Thanks be to God.

We pray for the whole church of Jesus in a world of turmoil and change where many feel lost and uncertain.

We pray for those seeking to stand up for goodness, to reaffirm the values of God's kingdom and the teaching of Christ as to how we should live.

Let us ask God for sensitive ways of being salt for the world.

The Lord hears our prayer.

Thanks be to God.

We pray for churches in places of violence and persecution; for those who are committed to standing alongside the poor, the broken, the defeated, the victims; for those congregations that are seeking to build bridges of hope and understanding in place of rejection, prejudice, and injustice.

The Lord hears our prayer.

Thanks be to God.

We pray for ourselves and for our worship, service, and mission, for the Spirit to lead us and his presence to fill us, for hope to encourage us and wisdom to teach us, for courage to serve Christ and the strength to love each other, for commitment to share our faith and God's love with our neighbor.

Let us ask God to fill us with the Holy Spirit for rebirth and renewal.

We bring our prayers in the name of the Lord of the church.
Amen.

· 79 ·

WARMTH AND PEACE

Father, we pray for those who take life and the things of life for
granted, for those who take others for granted and rarely show any
appreciation of what they receive, for those who make use of others and whose words and deeds affect the peace of their neighbor.

May Christ change the waters of their coldness with the wine of
his warmth and peace.

The Lord hears our prayer.

Thanks be to God.

Father, we pray for those who hide their pain and their fear,
their hurts and their sadness behind a mask of indifference, hard-
ness, and a pretence of self-confidence.

May Christ heal the waters of their brokenness with the wine of
his blessing and freedom.

The Lord hears our prayer.

Thanks be to God.

Father, we pray for those who are empty, lost, and afraid, for
those who once were active, alive, and involved but now simply
sit and watch and wait, for those who are now left to sit and stare,
and for those whose days have lost meaning and purpose, for those

who sit in the hospital and watch and long for someone to come, for those who have only their memories, and for those whose memories have all gone.

May Christ share the waters of their pain with his promise of the wine of eternal life.

The Lord hears our prayer.

Thanks be to God.

Father, we pray for any we know to be rejoicing, full of happiness and hope: for those soon to be married and for those who are facing the pressures of disharmony that have come with the years, for those who think only of what is needed for the wedding and forget that it will last just one day, for those who make no preparation for the giving, sharing, loving, and forgiving they will need in fulfilling the responsibility that their promises have laid upon them.

May Christ renew the waters of all our relationships with the wine of his joy and love.

The Lord hears our prayer.

Thanks be to God.

Father, we pray for any we know by name who are in particular need.

We name in our hearts those who are ill or in hospital, those who are facing an operation and afraid, those who are dying and those who care for them, those who are facing a time of stress at home or at work or with their family, those who are experiencing the loss of employment, the loss of someone they have loved, or the loss of any sense of direction in their lives, and those who have lost hope.

May Christ transform the water of their hurting with the wine of his compassion.

The Lord hears our prayer.

Thanks be to God.

In Christ's name. Amen.

· 80 ·

THE LIGHT OF CHRIST

Lord, we pray for wisdom for parents: for those under pressure or strain, for parents uncertain of employment and how to keep out of debt, for parents concerned for their children's welfare and future, and for those unconcerned or unaware of where their children are or what they are doing.

May the light of Christ be the source of wisdom for all parents.

In the name of Jesus, we ask our prayer.

We pray for wisdom for churches: for churches where the gospel is preached and faith in Christ is declared, for churches that have forgotten their reason for being and have degenerated into gatherings of human fellowship only, for churches that are so active in social concern, working with the young and the needy, that they have no time to pray or to study God's word, for churches rich in fellowship and the things of the Spirit but who never reach out with love or in mission.

May the light of Christ be the source of wisdom for all churches.

In the name of Jesus, we ask our prayer.

Lord, we pray for wisdom for all politicians: for those who came into politics with high ideals and a genuine desire to seek justice and truth, for those whose values and judgments are shaped by their knowledge of the Scriptures and their love of the Lord, for those whose only aim is to lift themselves higher, no matter the cost to their personal integrity, and for those who will sacrifice anything for their own personal gain.

May the light of Christ be the source of wisdom for all politicians.

In the name of Jesus, we ask our prayer. Amen.

81

WISDOM FOR OUR WORLD

Lord, we pray for wisdom for our world.

We pray for those who struggle for justice for the deprived and despairing, for those who are seeking to make the world a cleaner, safer, and fairer place for all, for governments that turn a blind eye to the effects of their decisions on our good world, for industrial leaders who give no thought of the impact on future generations that result from the profit-driven choices being made today.

May the light of Christ be the source of wisdom for all the world.

In the name of Jesus, we ask our prayer.

Lord, we pray for wisdom for people: for those trapped by the offer of instant solutions to their problems for today but who have no answer to the debts that must be faced tomorrow, for those enslaved by the false security offered by lotteries and for those who ignore the fact that sudden riches for some must be paid for by those who can least afford it, for those seeking to be faithful to Christ and the gospel of love in a world that has turned its back on its Maker.

May the light of Christ be the source of wisdom for all people.

In the name of Jesus, we ask our prayer.

Lord, we pray for wisdom for all young people: for those seeking guidance for their future studies and those still seeking employment in their chosen profession, for those finding it all but impossible just to say no in the face of pressure from their peers, and for those who have made Christ Lord of their hearts—may he also be Lord of their plans and dreams, their choices, and all their relationships.

We pray for young people whose lives and values are a challenge to all and for those whose lifestyle causes pain and despair to family and friends.

May the light of Christ be their source of wisdom.

In the name of Jesus, we ask our prayer.

We pray for wisdom for ourselves.

May the light of Christ be the source of our wisdom in all that

we face and in all that we choose, in all we plan and everything
we desire, in all our relationships and in all our service, in all our
commitments and all our obedience, in all our pain and in all our
pleasure, in all our successes and all our failures, in all our joys and in
all our sorrows, in our walking with God and trusting in Jesus, in our
waiting on the Spirit and in our surrender.

In the name of Jesus, we ask our prayer. Amen.

82

CALLED BY GOD

Father, we pray for the whole church, which you called into
being through your Son.

We are aware it was always your intention that your church
should be a blessing to all people everywhere.

We ask that by your Holy Spirit your church may be daily
renewed and empowered for the task for which you gave it life.

The Lord hears our prayer.

Thanks be to God.

We pray, Father, that we and all our fellow Christians may be
ready for any sacrifice, any action, any declaration that will clearly
demonstrate faith, hope, and love to our neighbors, our family
members, our friends, our coworkers, and our fellow journeyers.

The Lord hears our prayer.

Thanks be to God. Amen.

FALLEN WORLD

Lord, you have made us and loved us.

You designed us to live in fellowship with you and with each other.

May your infinite gentleness fill us with an assurance that you will hear us as we pray for your fallen, hurting world.

The Lord hears our prayer.

Thanks be to God.

Lord, we pray for this world in which so many people see you simply in terms of a remote power, a punishing God, someone to fear.

We pray for those who are angry, who are filled with a desire for revenge, for those whose bitterness has destroyed their lives.

The Lord hears our prayer.

Thanks be to God.

We pray for families whose love is being destroyed by jealousy, where people expect loving relationships simply to happen without any effort or commitment on their part each day.

May the love of God renew their hope and their striving for peace.

The Lord hears our prayer.

Thanks be to God.

We pray for children who suffer the consequences of their parents' failure to love and to care, for children whose lives are suffering the results of physical, mental, or sexual abuse.

May the caring, healing hand of Christ be upon them.

The Lord hears our prayer.

Thanks be to God. Amen.

· 84 ·

WITH PURPOSE

We pray for friends and neighbors, for those we work with, and for members of our own family who are without joy, hope, peace, or any real sense of purpose and direction in their lives.

May they know the revitalizing love of God.

The Lord hears our prayer.

Thanks be to God.

We pray for nations whose people are filled with hatred and aggression toward each other, for communities split by distrust and injustice.

May the love of God bring a deeper desire for true reconciliation.

We think particularly of [name of country].

The Lord hears our prayer.

Thanks be to God.

We pray for Christians who allow themselves to be divided from each other by church teaching or by their own narrow ideas.

Lord, we pray, break down the barriers we build between us, destroy the walls that keep us apart, that our oneness in the body of Christ might bring glory to his name and light to those in darkness.

The Lord hears our prayer.

Thanks be to God.

We pray for ourselves.

Lord, you know the things that make us stumble and fall, our weakness, our secret shame.

You know our words of faith and our feeble trust, our good intentions, and our faltering steps.

Lord, deliver us from evil, just as you promised to do.

Grant us wisdom, courage, gentleness and mercy, faith and love.

The Lord hears our prayer.

Thanks be to God.

The Lord hears all our prayers in the name of Christ our Lord. Amen.

85

FREEDOM TO LIVE

Father, we pray for all those who are suffering and enslaved.

We pray especially for those who see no hope, no new beginning, no relief or freedom, for those who today are suffering political oppression, persecution, or imprisonment because of their faith in Christ.

May the hope of Christ set them free.

Lord, in your mercy, hear our prayer.

We pray for all victims of violence, for all who are despised or rejected, for all who are diminished or frustrated by illness, pain, illiteracy, or poverty.

We pray for all who are slaves to addiction: eating or drinking to excess or addicted to smoking, gambling, or illegal drugs.

May the power of Christ set them free.

Lord, in your mercy, hear our prayer.

We pray for all oppressors: for all leaders and governments who dare not give their people freedom to think, act, or choose for themselves, for all who are making other people's lives miserable, for those who exploit other people's weaknesses and fears.

May the truth of Christ set them free.

Lord, in your mercy, hear our prayer.

We pray for all relationships where there is a desire to dominate: for families that are ruled by authoritarian parents or where children receive no proper discipline, for relationships where emotional blackmail is used to gain power or control over each other, for those who are never allowed to blossom, to be free, to be the people they were meant to be.

May the joy of Christ set them free.

Lord, in your mercy, hear our prayer.

We pray for all who have been crushed by insensitive words or damaged by unthinking actions, for those broken by lies, abuse, or the lack of unconditional love, for all without hope, peace, or the ability to love and be loved.

May the love of Christ set them free.

Lord, in your mercy, hear our prayer.

We pray for those who sigh and cry for freedom, for those who long to know that the past is dealt with, the future is in God's hands, and today is his gift to us all.

We pray for those who hold the broken, share the pain of the hurting, and walk with those who are lost.

May the mercy of Christ set them free.

Lord, in your mercy, hear our prayer.

We pray for ourselves.

Let us ask Christ to touch our thoughts, our words, and our dreams.

Let us pray that every corner of our lives might be open to his will; that his love and truth will give us hope, and his presence will fill us with joy.

Let us ask for the power of the Spirit to light up our lives with peace and understanding.

May the light of Christ set us free.

Lord, in your mercy, hear our prayer.

In the name of Christ, who sets us free. Amen.

86

LIFE FOR THE WORLD

I am a young person.

I am told that I have everything too easy today, not like when older generations were young.

I know drugs are bad news; that I need to work hard because my future depends on it.

But you do not understand the pressures inside, at home, and with my friends.

There is no one to talk to, no one I feel I can trust.

I want to know what life really means.

Pray for me.

[Silence]

I am an old person.

It's not being old that I mind so much; it's being ignored and made to feel I do not matter any more.

I spend so much time on my own these days.

I feel trapped in my house and few people visit me now.

My friends have all gone and my family live so far away.

I just want to talk about how life used to be.

Pray for me.

[Silence]

I am a parent.

I always wanted a family.

It has been a great joy to watch them grow up and become independent.

But as they have grown, they have at times been a great worry and are a continuing concern.

I find it hard to cope with their friends, their music, and their attitudes.

I wonder sometimes if I put them first too often and how life will feel when they finally leave home.

Pray for me.

[Silence]

I am a single person.

Whether I am single by my own choice or because of my situation, I still feel excluded by our family-oriented society.

I am made to feel different, and sometimes it seems that people avoid me.

It costs more being single, and there's no one to share life's good times and bad.

There's no one to wish you goodnight or good morning; to be there when you come home.

Pray for me.

[Silence]

I am a retired person.

I have good memories of the colleagues with whom I shared all those years.

It was all very stressful and the work was constantly changing, but now that it is gone I miss the daily routine and the value it all gave.

That the end came when I did not expect it made it harder to bear.

Now each day is the same and I must learn a new way of living and finding my worth.

Pray for me.

[Silence]

I am a prisoner.

Whether my prison has bars and a jailer or I am just trapped by a life that is hurting, I still long to be free.

Whether my prison has walls of abuse or addictions I can't break, whether they are real or just in my head, whether my prison is built on my fears, my anxiety, or my ill health, I still need to be set free.

I just want to live and learn to be me.

Pray for me.

[Silence]

I am a church member.

I have believed in God virtually all of my life.

I have never not believed.

I have always enjoyed the hymns, the prayers, and the fellowship each Sunday.

I found serving the church and the community a natural expression of my faith in God.

But I have never had my heart strangely warmed by his presence and the power of the Spirit.

For the first time in my life I want to be made new.

Pray for me.

[Silence]

Lord, in your mercy, hear our prayer.

In Christ's name. Amen.

87

TEMPTATION

We pray for those whose lives are crippled by prejudice, self-satisfaction, and fear, for those who are deaf to the cries of the hungry and the starving, and for those who blame those less fortunate for things over which they have had little or no control.

May the love of Christ soften hardened hearts.

The Lord hears our prayer.

Thanks be to God.

We pray for those whose lives are full of guilt, real or imagined, for those who feel unable to forgive themselves for the things they have said or done or failed to do, for those filled with remorse, for those who do not see how they can put their lives back together again, for those who have given in to temptation so many times their consciences have become hardened.

May the gentle voice of Christ reach into the depths of their need.

The Lord hears our prayer.

Thanks be to God.

We pray for those who seek to manipulate other people and for those who rely on emotional blackmail to get their own way, for parents who neglect appropriate discipline of their children and those who abuse their position of trust, for those who have never known what it means to be loved unconditionally, and for those who long to know they are accepted.

May the patience of Christ bring hope where it is most needed.

The Lord hears our prayer.

Thanks be to God.

We pray for those who long to have faith, for those who have yet to realize that it cannot be achieved, only received as a gift from God's hand, for those who, because they have faith in God, think that this is an excuse for not using their God-given powers of thought and reason, for those whose faith is fragile and weak and is soon lost in the heat of temptation.

May the safe hands of Christ give strength to those in danger of falling.

The Lord hears our prayer.

Thanks be to God.

In the name of Christ. Amen.

. 88 .

Facing Conflict

I ask your prayers for all who face conflict, for those for whom life is an endless struggle, for those who are uncertain where their next meal will come from, or if it will come at all, for those whom life seems dark and empty, for all who are hungry in our greedy world, for those sent away from the rich nations' table empty-handed, although there is enough for all.

The Lord hears our prayer.

Thanks be to God.

I ask your prayers for all who face conflict; for those who are persecuted, all who are tortured and imprisoned for their faith in Christ, for all who are neglected, ignored, made to feel as if they do not count, for those who for the sake of others stand against injustice, corruption, and evil and do so at great cost to themselves.

The Lord hears our prayer.

Thanks be to God.

I ask your prayers for all who face conflict: for homes where life is one long argument, where the members of families cannot agree, for relationships that began in love and hope but have been soured by broken promises, and trust has been lost, for those facing violence, hatred, or indifference, for those who long ago were robbed of their innocence, and for those hurting still.

The Lord hears our prayer.

Thanks be to God.

I ask your prayers for all who face conflict: for those who have a conflict within, for those who find it hard to love or be loved because they have never been loved from the first, for those whose lives are in turmoil, yet the smile on their face hides the hurt and the pain deep inside, for those filled with a sense of loss and with sadness, for those for whom the bottom has dropped out of their world, for those filled with anger and bitterness, for those crushed with doubts and fears, for those with no sense of their own value and no joy in the friendship of others because they are locked up in themselves.

The Lord hears our prayer.

Thanks be to God.

I ask your prayers for all who face conflict: for those facing conflicts within the church, for those who are disturbed by change and resist anything that is new or different, for churches that settle for what has always been and refuse to allow the life-renewing Spirit to set them free to work, witness, and serve God in new ways and in the words of today, for those who are so committed to guarding the unchanging and unchangeable good news that they neglect or refuse to discover the way it must be told to make it relevant for today's world.

The Lord hears our prayer.

Thanks be to God.

I ask your prayers for all whose lives have no conflict: for those who have settled for second best, for those who are determined to be secret disciples of Christ, silent witnesses for God, for those who refuse to be different and are content to blend in with the crowd, for those who were called to be faithful to God, daring for

Christ and alive with the Spirit but have buried it all deep inside in case others should know; for those who have no conflict—except with their Lord.

The Lord hears our prayer.

Thanks be to God.

I ask your prayers for all who have conflict: for those whose sickness has broken their spirit and for those whose ill-health has worn them down, for those whose illness has restricted the lives of their families, for those who have lost their freedom as they are concerned for the old and infirm, for all who take up the battle to bring wholeness, healing, renewal, and hope, for all who are committed to prayer and to love.

The Lord hears our prayer.

Thanks be to God.

We bring our prayers in the name of Christ, who shares all our conflicts. Amen.

89

JESUS THE TEACHER

Father, we pray for those who teach others: for all involved in all aspects of education, for those who teach in day schools, in colleges of further education, or in universities.

May they have wisdom, integrity, and a commitment to share all that is good and true and right.

Lord, in your mercy, hear our prayer.

We pray for those who are taught: for children and young people, for those just beginning school and those now planning their future, for those studying away from home for the first time in their lives and for those still trying to use all they have been taught.

May they discover that learning is more than just information and life is bigger than all they have been given.

Lord, in your mercy, hear our prayer.

We pray for those whose words and actions influence others.

We pray for all involved in the media: for television producers and newspaper editors, for writers and poets and all entertainers, for sports men and women and all whose lifestyle becomes a role model for others.

May they speak and act with an awareness of the responsibility that is placed on their shoulders.

Lord, in your mercy, hear our prayer.

We pray for those whose words and deeds affect many people: for leaders of nations, of unions, and industry, for all members of our own government.

Lord, we pray that you will keep them aware of the impact their decisions and actions have for people everywhere and the huge implications for generations to come.

Lord, in your mercy, hear our prayer.

We pray for those whose words touch and change the attitudes and lives of others: for those in the police force, for judges, prison officials, prison chaplains, probation officers, and for those who work for victims. May they have wisdom and understanding to balance freedom and justice and mercy for all.

Lord, in your mercy, hear our prayer.

We pray for all church leaders and preachers and those with pastoral responsibility in the church or the community, for members of all churches all over the world, for parents and colleagues, for families and friends.

Keep them aware of the unique potential of each person they meet.

Lord, in your mercy, hear our prayer.

We pray for ourselves.

Lord, touch our words and our deeds; change our thoughts and our attitudes; transform our values and our intentions.

May the way we respond to others and to all the challenges of life bring you praise and glory and draw others to Christ.

Lord, in your mercy, hear our prayer.

In Christ's name. Amen.

· 90 ·

THOSE WHO ARE SUFFERING

We pray for those who suffer because of the actions of others: for those whose lives are damaged through someone's neglect or whose future plans are wrecked by someone's thoughtlessness, for those who started with such high hopes only to see them thrown into the dust, and for those whose trust in other people has been broken because those in whom they put their faith have let them down.

May they know the suffering Christ shares in their pain.

The Lord hears our prayer.

Thanks be to God.

We pray for those who suffer because of their own foolishness: for those whose addictions to illegal drugs and to alcohol are wrecking their lives, their relationships, and their future and are also spoiling the lives of those nearest to them, for those whose selfishness, greed, and self-centered ambitions have separated them from friends and family, and for those who have deliberately chosen what they knew was wrong and are now paying the price for their carelessness.

May they know that the powerful arms of God are always around them.

The Lord hears our prayer.

Thanks be to God.

We pray for those who suffer because of their experience of grief, for those who have lost someone they love and have no one to share it with and for those whose hearts are heavy and aching and there seems to be no one who understands, for those who are finding it hard to cope with their sadness and sorrow and those overwhelmed with their grief and their feelings of guilt, for those who are filled with regrets for what they did or failed to do, and for those who do not see how they can put their lives back together again.

May they know the compassion of Christ and the peace of God.

The Lord hears our prayer.

Thanks be to God.

We pray for those who suffer because of unjust governments and oppressive regimes: for those imprisoned for their faith in Christ and for those who suffer torture, house arrest, and harassment because they dare to challenge their political leaders and to stand on the side of the poor, for those imprisoned without trial, and for those rejected and hated even by family and friends because of their commitment to Christ and their obedience to God's will.

May they know the hope and the joy of God in their hearts.

The Lord hears our prayer.

Thanks be to God.

We pray for those who suffer because of their experience of loss: for those who have lost their job and with it their sense of purpose and pattern each day and those who are facing financial problems through no fault of their own; for those who have been required to take early retirement and feel rejected, inferior, and unwanted, and those who feel broken and useless because they have lost all meaning and status in life; for those whose work cripples their lives; for those who are square pegs in round holes; and for those who feel trapped in employment that is slowly wrecking their lives and their homes.

May they know the presence of Christ in all they face this week.

The Lord hears our prayer.

Thanks be to God.

We pray for those who suffer through illness: for those whose lives have lost all their fitness and strength and whose joy in life is being sapped away, for those whose sickness is lifelong and cannot be cured, for those with a terminal illness, and for those who suffer with them and care for them and feel helpless to do anything good.

May they know the love of God that makes them whole.

The Lord hears our prayer.

Thanks be to God.

We pray for those who suffer because of their poverty: those who are hungry and starving to death in a world of God's plenty and those who consume an unfair share of the world's resources, keeping others poor and in want, for those who are longing for rain to heal the parched earth and water their crops and those who watch their children suffer and die and are helpless to do anything to save them.

May the grace of God move the hearts of the rich and the comfortable to help those in great need.

The Lord hears our prayer.

Thanks be to God.

We pray for those who are facing any kind of trouble, anxiety, fear, or doubt, for those suffering from the pressures and demands laid upon them and those for whom the burden of responsibility is too much to bear, for churches whose property is vandalized and those struggling to bear their witness in a society that just does not want to know, for churches and Christians who are genuinely seeking to love their neighbor and to name the name of Christ.

We pray for ourselves and all we are facing in our lives right now and all we must face in the coming days of the week.

May the presence of God guide and help us still.

The Lord hears our prayer.

Thanks be to God.

Prayers of Commitment

· 91 ·

THE LOVE OF CHRIST

Lord, you call us to be loving; you challenge us to care; you enable us to share your grace.

We commit ourselves to be open to you in all things.

By your Holy Spirit, give us the power and the will to demonstrate the love of Christ in all we say and do and are.

In Christ's name. Amen.

· 92 ·

GIVE US WISDOM

Lord, you have called us to know you, to love you, and to serve you.

You have made us your own and filled us with your grace.

We commit ourselves to be open to your word, to listen to your voice, and to be guided by your Spirit.

We pray, give us the wisdom, strength, and courage to trust you, obey you, and walk with you all our days.

For Christ's sake. Amen.

· 93 ·

CHOSEN AND CALLED

Lord, you have chosen and called us to worship and serve you and to open our lives to the power of your word.

You have loved us and healed us.

You have changed us and filled us.

Now set us free to be signs of your grace to those who are lost and to those who are hurting.

We commit ourselves to Christ and to be open to your will.

Now fill us with your Spirit that we may live in the freedom of your grace. Amen.

· 94 ·

SENT IN HIS NAME

Father, you have loved us and saved us.

You have held us and healed us and made our lives whole.

You have given us new hope and new life.

You have filled us with your Spirit and fed us with your word.

You have called us in Christ.

Now send us in your name to serve you and glorify you forever. Amen.

· 95 ·

LIVING IN THE WILDERNESS

Father, we are only too well aware that the world is full of wilderness experiences.

We commit ourselves to love those in need of affection, to hold those who are hurting, to listen to those who are lonely, to speak the truth to those who are mistaken, to stand with those who are standing alone, and to walk with those who have lost their way home.

Give us your compassion, your wisdom, your strength, and your victory that we may be Christ to our neighbor. Amen.

· 96 ·

STEPS OF FAITH

Loving, generous God, you gave your Son to live and die for us all.

You did this, not because we deserve it, but because you love us.

Lord, by your Holy Spirit, enable us to take steps of faith, hope, and love that the name of Christ might be lifted up and people everywhere might join in the song of praise to him. Amen.

· 97 ·

POWER FOR THE TASK

Father, you are the source, guide, and goal of all life.

You have given us responsibility not only for our own lives but also for the well-being of our neighbor.

We ask you to fill us with the love and power of your Spirit that we may complete the task you have laid upon us.

In Jesus' name. Amen.

· 98 ·

STRENGTHENED BY CHRIST

We can go, because he came.

We can be sent, because he goes with us.

We can stand, because he is Lord.

We can do all things in Christ who gives us the strength. Amen.

· 99 ·

OVERFLOWING WITH THE SPIRIT

Father, when there is a cross, we will carry it; when we pass through despair, we will endure it; when our peace is broken, we will suffer it; when we mourn, we will do it bravely; when we are overwhelmed, we will bear it trusting in your promises alone.

Whatever we face, whatever happens, wherever we go, keep us true to you, filled with Christ and overflowing with the Spirit. Amen.

· 100 ·

LISTENING FOR GOD

Lord, you are the word of God and you have the Word of life for us all.

You are the source of hope, joy, and life for us.

Speak to our hearts those words we need to hear that our words and deeds may find new life in you. Amen.

· 101 ·

TOUCHED BY CHRIST

Father, you called us out of our darkness and into your light.

You have taken away our emptiness and filled us with Christ.

You have touched our pain and made us whole.

You have shared our suffering and made it your own.

You have loved us and held us, and you walk with us still.

You have blessed us and healed us and made us your children.

You have become our Savior—we now call you Lord.

You have called us—now send us to live and to love and serve your world. Amen.

· 102 ·

COMMITTING OURSELVES

Lord, we commit ourselves to listen for your voice, to trust your word, to speak your name, to live for your glory, and to honor you in all we say and do and are.

For Christ's sake. Amen.

· 103 ·

LORD, GO WITH US

Living Lord, go with us into the world.

Stand by us when we are weak, hold us and save us from falling, love us in spite of our sin, and fill our lives with the power of your resurrection that we may be channels of your light in our neighbor's darkness. Amen.

Prayers of Benediction

104

SONG OF PRAISE

Lord, we commit ourselves to continue the song of praise that we have shared together and to live in the spirit of thankfulness that we have declared.

We commit ourselves to be the people of prayer that we have sought to be and to be open to your word every day of our lives.

We ask that you will so fill us with your Holy Spirit that our changed hearts, our transformed lives, and our declarations of the love of God may lead others to place their faith in you and give you all the glory.

Through Christ our Lord. Amen.

105

WE ARE YOUR PEOPLE

Lord, we are your people.

You have called us by name and lavished your love upon us.

We go now bearing your name on our lips and your love in our lives.

As your people, may we so live and speak that our neighbors will give thanks to God and their lives to Christ. Amen.

· 106 ·
WHATEVER WE FACE

Whatever we face, we do not face it alone.

Wherever we go, we do not journey alone.

However we suffer, we do not bear it alone.

Whoever we are and wherever we go and however we journey, we go in peace, in hope, and in faith for we go with Christ, who always goes with us. Amen.

· 107 ·
HAVE NO FEAR

Have no fear; Christ has overcome the world.

Have no doubt; he has promised to be with you.

Have no anxiety; he is Lord, and we shall share his joy, his life, his love, and his victory. Amen.

· 108 ·

WE CAME IN WEAKNESS

We came in weakness; we go in strength.

We came alone; we go together.

We came in brokenness; we go in wholeness.

We came with our questions; we go knowing Christ is the answer.

We came for a Savior; we go with a Lord.

We came empty-handed; we go with hearts filled.

We came defeated, lost, and full of selfishness and sin; we go forgiven, found, and in the victory of Christ.

We go because he sends us.

We go because he fills us.

We go because he goes with us. Amen.

· 109 ·

ASKING AND OFFERING

Lord, we have asked for your mercy; help us to offer it to others.

Lord, we have sought your forgiveness; enable us to share it with others.

Lord, we have received your love; help us to show it to others.

Lord, we have experienced your joy; make us examples of hope for others.

Lord, we have received your peace; make us channels of peace to our neighbors.

Lord, we have worshipped you here; send us out to praise you everywhere.

Lord, we have trusted you here and shared our faith in you in this place; now go with us that our commitment to Christ may bring forth fruits of love, hope, joy, and peace for our neighbor.

In the name of him who calls and sends us. Amen.

· 110 ·

LORD, WITH YOUR HELP

Lord, with your help, we shall not fail you.

With your presence, we shall be strong.

With your light, we shall conquer the darkness.

With your love, we shall be free.

With your Spirit, we shall have the power to bring you glory and honor and praise. Amen.

· 111 ·

CHANNELS OF GRACE

Lord, you have brought us to this moment in our lives.

We look back and give thanks for all you have done for us and for being with us no matter what.

We look forward to all we must face in the future in the knowledge of your promise to be with us always.

So today we commit ourselves to be open to you and to be channels of your grace to all we meet.

Lord, loosen our tongues and open our hearts, and by the power of your Holy Spirit enable us to be faithful witnesses for Christ. Amen.

112

LORD, THE JOURNEY IS HARD

Lord, the journey is hard, and we do not know the turnings.

The path is difficult, and we can easily lose our way.

The way you have prepared for us is narrow and often tests us.

Give us your peace, courage, and guidance and an assurance of your living presence to the end and beyond. Amen.

113

SHARING THE HURT

Lord, we know that you have never promised that life would be easy and trouble free.

We are aware that you promised that following you would involve carrying a cross.

We commit ourselves to trust you and to walk with you for you have promised to walk with us to the end and beyond.

We commit ourselves to share in the hurt and the pain of others and to hold them in Christ's love and in his name. Amen.

· 114 ·

LORD, WHEN THINGS GO WELL

Lord, when things go well or our world falls apart, we will be your people.

When we are alone or in a crowd, we will be your people.

When we are full and when we are empty, we will be your people.

When we feel lost, afraid, or broken, we will be your people.

Wherever we go and whatever we face, we will be your people.

Lord, fill us with your Spirit that we may live for your glory and as the people of God. Amen.

· 115 ·

WE CAME ALONE

We came alone; we go together.

We came in doubt and fear; we go in hope and courage.

We came in sin and shame; we go in the assurance of God's love.

We came in emptiness; we go because we have been filled. Amen.

· 116 ·

OUR CONFIDENCE IN CHRIST

Lord, no longer will we put our trust in ourselves, nor will we place our hope in our own skills, strength, and ability.

We will not rely on our possessions for our security, nor will we trust anyone but you to make us whole.

Lord, we commit ourselves to trust you and to put our confidence in Christ alone. Amen.

· 117 ·

LORD, SEND US OUT

Lord, send us out in the name of Christ; fill us with your love and mercy.

By your Holy Spirit enable us so to live and speak that your love and joy may flow into every corner of life.

We go in your name.

We go in your love.

We go for the glory of your holy name. Amen.

· 118 ·

In the Quietness

Lord, in the quietness, touch our lives and hold us fast.

Lord, in the stillness, share our hurt and our sense of aloneness.

Lord, in our weakness, be strength for us.

Lord, in our darkness, be our light and our hope.

Lord, in our doubts, be our courage and faith.

Lord, in our need, be our Savior and friend.

Lord, in our lives, be our reason for living.

Lord, be our source of life and our fulfillment and joy.

Lord, be the meaning in our service and our obedience.

Lord, be at the heart of our worship and celebration.

Lord, be our Lord, here and everywhere, until the end and beyond. Amen.

· 119 ·

We Know That We Are Yours

Lord, we know that we are yours because you have made us your own.

We belong to your kingdom because your Spirit tells us that it is so.

We go in the knowledge of your peace, hope, joy, and truth to live as citizens of your heavenly kingdom. Amen.

· 120 ·

GO WITH US FROM THIS PLACE

Go with us from this place, Lord, for we cannot serve, trust, and live for you in our own strength.

Go with us, Lord, for you are the true and living way.

Go with us, Lord, that we may walk with you. Amen.

My Prayers

_____

_____

_____

_____

_____

_____

_____

_____

_____

_____

_____

_____

_____

_____

_____

_____

_____

_____

_____

_____

_____

_____

_____

_____

_____

_____

_____

_____

_____

_____

_____

Index